Hurricane Drinking

This is my story of the two hurricanes that Hurricane Maria. It is the first time 2 categ .... a two-week period and it is the first time something like this happened in the Virgin Islands. St. Croix, where I live, has, for decades, been defined by Hurricane Hugo; a colossal storm that terrorized the island in 1989. There is a healthy debate going on as to whether Hugo or now Maria was more debilitating to the island. I'll leave that to the meteorologists and historians to decide. This book is one person's experience of surviving a Category 5 hurricane and its aftermath. Everything here is true. It happened to my family. That said, it doesn't represent everyone's story. It's not supposed to do that. By so many standards, we were lucky. We lived. We were able to stay in our own home. We weren't rich but we were able to have enough resources to survive the melee that followed the storm. Many of my fellow islanders were not so lucky. So I offer this up as a snapshot into a natural catastrophic event and what followed as something you may never experience in your life (and I hope you don't) and how we survived.

The book is set up in an unusual way. Hurricane Irma is a short story. While it reeked horrible damage on many parts of the Caribbean; we were spared most of its wrath. So, my writing about it seemed more confined to a short story. The next section of the book is about Hurricane Maria and the, more or less 6 hours she danced around St. Croix. Most of the Maria story is humorous (you'll recognize what's not) and that is because, I have found, that humor is the greatest form of relief. It doesn't mean that we laughed our way through the storm or the aftermath, but it does mean, in hindsight, I can see some of this humorously. I again want to emphasize that I don't mean any disrespect for lives lost or people who have minimally or haven't rebuilt their lives. Hurricanes are terrible events and cause countless disruptions to lives and property. What I will say that's good is the bond it has forged with friends and family who have lived through it or supported us through it. It is really true; you find out who has your back when you're in a foxhole.

Hurricane Drinking

The Preamble

My husband and I moved to sunny St. Croix in 2013 from New York. It was one of the worst winters on record in New York (see a pattern here?) and we couldn't wait to pack our bags and head south. My husband came down first to the house we had bought—the proverbial worse house in a great neighborhood. It wasn't the first time we'd done this. In fact, our house in New Rochelle, New York had been the same scenario. What distinguished our house in St. Croix is that we would be remodeling it on an island. As my husband likes to say, we bought a fixer-upper and we've been fixing it and upping it ever since. But I digress......

Frank, my husband, moved in November. I stayed in New York and focused on selling the house there. He made the unforgiveable sin of calling me during one of the artic blasts and said, 'hey the weather is really amazing here; how is it there?' I'm certain the occasional deafness he suffers is a direct result of my response.

Before you wonder, what kind of people pack up and move to a Caribbean island (and there are LOTS); let me share with you that my husband and I had been vacationing on St. Croix for almost 20 years. We knew the island. The irony is not lost on us that despite that frequency, the first hurricane we ever experienced, until Maria, was in New York. Hurricane Sandy hit when we were living there. (Again, what's with the weather patterns?) We lost our power then for 10 days. Remember that number; it will be important later and there will be a test. We thought we knew what to expect. We were about to find out differently.

Table of Contents

Hurricane One: Hurricane Irma

Hurricane Two: Hurricane Maria

Chapter One: The Prep

Chapter Two: Generators and the Fine Art of Auto Mechanics

Chapter Three: Coke Addiction

Chapter Four: Hometown Heroes Hurricanes and Paper Towels

Chapter Five: B&B or Hurricane Refugee Center

Chapter Six: Electrical Wires, Sink Holes and Crappy Roads

Chapter Seven: Power

Chapter Eight: Hurricane Sex

Chapter Nine: Refrigerators and Why You Don't Need Them (just kidding)

Chapter Ten: Hurricane Diet

Chapter Eleven: The USPS

Chapter Twelve: Am I Coming or Am I Going?

Chapter Thirteen: Beast of Burden

Chapter Fourteen: Relief Workers

Chapter Fifteen: The ABCs of Relief

Chapter Sixteen: Hurricane Drinking

Epilogue

Hurricane One—Irma

"See you on the other side," said each person as they kissed and hugged each other.

I did it too even though everyone knows I don't hug. It's become somewhat of a game to get me to hug for those "in the know".

But not this night. This night, I'm hugging and kissing with the best of them. This night is the night before, Hurricane Irma, the largest hurricane in recorded history in the Caribbean, is on track to hit the US Virgin Islands—where I live.

This gathering of people at Ziggy's, our local gas station/bar/grocery store/community center, is my family. They are my uncle that drives me nuts; the siblings who know everything about me and love me anyway; understanding parents and disappointing children. In this group, all of those are represented. It's an unusual group of people who make their permanent home an island. While we do our share of drinking, with all deference to Jimmy Buffett, we're not 'wasted away again in Margaritaville'. Some of us must work.

Living on an island, I've said a million times is like living in a small town. So, expect everyone to know your business. There's also a segregation between part-timers and full-timers. While part-timers love the life; full-timers love the island.

But I digress.

This night we seem reluctant to leave. We were taking mental photos….in case.

That afternoon, when my husband and I had done the last of our hurricane prep; sitting on our deck, he looked at me thoughtfully and said, 'we won't rebuild it back this way". It was the first time either of us had acknowledged that our beautiful home, might not make it.

The owners of Ziggy's, who had worked hard all day securing the place, were anxious to leave and get home to their own families.

"Go, leave," became the refrain from each of them.

My husband and I pulled away from the last friend, intently staring in our eyes and vowing, "'let's check on each other". We worked our way through the twinge of cars and joined forces on the other side.

We are each other's rock, but that never seemed more important than that night. We trusted each other's skills and competency; we just didn't want to put it to the test.

The street lights faded in the background as we drove home, the now familiar path. We were both quiet—to be expected. Lost in our thoughts, tense as barbed wired, we moved stiffly from the car.

"I'll get the wingnuts," he said, his voice fading as he walked.

We'd saved the last duty for now. Putting up the metal shutters that overlap each other over our doors with windows. We'd never done it before and there was a sense of finality; like we were sealing our own tomb.

The winds had started to pick up and what had been a sticky, hot day had suddenly become cooler. The irony of the reason was not lost on me. Each billow of air lifted a slick piece of hair off the back of my neck and provided momentary relief. As we screwed the last wingnut in place, I looked around at this home, we had poured so much into. A house that had once been ugly and abandoned and now was improved and much loved. A home my neighbor called a "happy home".

"We won't rebuild it back this way."

Those words echoed in my head. There have been few Category 5 hurricanes on record, and one was coming our way.

All the hurricane prep manuals give you very detailed instructions about how to prepare.
1. Bottled water
2. Non-perishable foods—think Campbell soup
3. All your important documents in one water-proof place—that implies lots of water
4. Gas for the generator
5. Gas for your cars
6. Food for your pets
7. Flashlights
8. Clean clothes
9. Prescriptions

There's more, but that's the basics.

What the list doesn't say is this.
1. Get rid of your hysterical island friends on Facebook. You don't need that added stress.

I lost track of the number of FB friends I stopped following because of their constant stream of hysteria!

2. Do drugs. I don't care if it's medicinal marijuana or valium—do something.

You cannot use mechanical tools if your hands are shaking too bad. Now that I think of it; maybe if you just do well at #1, you won't need #2.

3. Be sure you're with someone you trust.

I can't emphasize this enough. Staring at the possibility of dying, better be for a good cause or with someone you know has your back. Not the gooey-eyed support but the "I'll keep you from flying into a wall" support.

We are again dawdling as we go inside. We're moving to our first-floor bedroom and away from our gorgeous Master Bedroom. This room is solid concrete; where all our electronics sit; has its own bathroom and, most important, is 20 steps from the front door—in case we must flee.

My husband digests as many sleeping pills as is safe and available. I try to sleep but keep jolting awake with violent dreams of concrete cracking and roofs flying away. At 3:00 am, I give up and lay in bed and listen to the silence. The usual cacophony of tree frogs and thrashers and other night creatures is absent. It's as if they never existed.

As dawn breaks, I hear the rustling of my husband beside me and the nervous morning twitches of our Vizsla, who thinks we're on a camping trip in our house. Like a small child, we've worked to protect him from our fears.

It's 6:00 a.m. I harness the dog up with his short leash, my oldest sister's advice ringing in my ears, "make sure you have a sturdy leash and harness". We make like our usual routine and he prances out the door; although instead of turning left for his morning walk, we turn right. My goal is to get him to pee. That is all. We've been told the hurricane will last between 3-10 hours. Meteorology, despite what you've been told, is not an exact science. They are predicting 180-225 mph winds. She's a Cat 5, with the fury and fire of the worst storm in recorded history in the Caribbean. That's what we hear the night before. She's mad and she's coming our way.

My husband goes out to check on the generator. We've agreed we're going to be judicious with its use. Couple hours on/ couple hours off. The conversation had been timely. By early morning, the power is gone. Rumors are swirling on social media that the government is going to shut down the utilities to preserve energy.

He trudges out and flips the switch to return us to power. A chore he will dutifully repeat numerous times over the next several days.

I've prepared my family. I sent a text message to my siblings the night before. In case.

> So, I wish I had better news, but it looks like Irma is going to do some damage. It's still not projected to come over us but with damaging winds up to 45 miles wide, it can still inflict some pain and from the looks of it, it's going to. She's going to be a Cat 4 when she plows through

here.

I wish I could sugar coat it but I don't think I should. We're as prepared as we can be and that's all we can do. If you have an iPhone, there is an app by the Red Cross that I've registered us with, so you can check on us. If we lose power and cell service, I'll stay in touch the best I can for as long as I can. The first of the storm arrives tomorrow.

The first of the responses was immediate.

Are you crazy?

I knew who it was from and why she sent it.

Have you ever known me to exaggerate?

Even though service interruption had been a given—even the night before, I had cell phone reception.

It's the truth

That was what I sent back when there was no reply.

No sense in keeping it from her.

That was last night.

I'd loaded up the weather channel on the computer and with the hum of the generator we both went back to social media.

"Did you see this?"

"Yea, I read that one."

"Hey wait."

"What did he just say?"

Our heads swivel in unison to the talking head who said she'd turned. We didn't even have to know who "she" is in their conversation. We know.

"I found it. She's turned 10 degrees."

We look at each other. Should we be hopeful? Is that relief in his eyes?

We keep digging.

Social media is plastered with the same thing. Everyone posting the same words.
> We're going to lose power.
> We're going to lose cell phone service.
> We're going to be fine.
> We're going to be fine.

We won't rebuild it back this way.

She's turned.

Social media is giddy with the prospect, well some of us are giddy.

St. Croix is going to miss the full impact, but she didn't turn deep enough or soon enough. St. Thomas and St. John are going to get it.

It's almost 1:00 pm in the afternoon and the worst of the winds and the wind gusts are over us and they are noisy. The dog is snoring. Despite little activity, he's bored, so he's sleeping.

My nerves and exhaustion are turning to tired. My eyes droop. I'm wired but relieved.

She turned.

By 2:30 p.m., I'm asleep. I sleep fitfully through, what I later learn are some of the most damaging winds.

My adrenaline has circled my emotions and decreed me done.

I wake up sweaty, despite the air conditioning and spent.

My phone beeps.

Despite 75 mph gusts, we have cell phone coverage.

We won't rebuild it back the same way.

I roll over and see my husband scrolling through news stories on his phone.

"She's mostly gone," he announces. "Your phone just went off."

I pad to the bath room where my phone is charging thanks to our generator. It's my sister.

> Are you o.k.?

Am I ok?

I see the peaceful scene of my dog sleeping and my husband relaxing on our bed.

> We're good

Which is true in so many ways.

> *O.k. well this all seems weird, but I love you.*
>
> *To me too. Love you too.*

We ride out the rest of the day listening to the winds howl and the intermittent rain pours.

She turned. She turned 10 degrees and spared us.

By the next day, we start hearing reports of the devastation that happened to our sister islands—St. Thomas and St. John. Complaints about electricity and phone service seem petty.

Despite the odds.

Despite her fury.

We were spared.

We were spared.

We won't have to worry about how to rebuild.

We won't have to rebuild.

Hurricane Two—Maria

Chapter 1

The Prep

This storm was different. We knew, because it had only happened two weeks before, how to board up the house. I'm not going to lie; we were in somewhat of disbelief that another major hurricane was heading our way. The second week after Irma, we had been in business meetings with other island business owners, counting our blessings that we had come through relatively unscathed and discussing ways to capitalize on that for our island. It was, to say the least, surreal.

We were concerned, the storm was only a 2 and it seemed like it might be ok. That's what we told ourselves. While we had lost power for only a couple of days after Irma, many of our friends still didn't have power back. Utilities on an island can be somewhat iffy and our island was no different.

We know we should be doing our hurricane prep but instead we're selling our wares to a cruise ship that was diverted from St. Martin because of Hurricane Irma. There is a small but determined group of business owners, who are committed to make lemonade out of the lemons the rest of the islands were handed. St. Croix had been an amazing tourist attraction until 29 years ago when Hurricane Hugo decimated the island. Since then cruise ships and airlines have bypassed the big island for sexier, smaller ones.

The cruise ship that came today was small, just 4,000 people. The island planned and pulled together well in a short amount of time. For my husband and I, it was a waste of time. Most of them were looking for cheaper items, so we leave hot, exhausted and not much richer. We're happy for some of the businesses and we see this as a turn for our sleepy island. "We're the only one still standing in the Caribbean" becomes the mantra. People are printing shirts and planning for, the inevitable onslaught of cruise ships. How else could it be? We fall into bed tired, but hopeful.

Monday

I'm awake early. I'm wired but not quite sure why. After Irma, the hurricane prep should go quicker because we've got the routine. We start systematically moving plants and patio furniture—filling every nook and cranny of our laundry room and electrical room; leaving just enough room in the electrical room for my husband to reach the electrical panel to engage the generator when we need it. There's not a question of if; it's when. Despite the varying prediction of the size of the storm, we're certain the government will shut the grid down to protect it.

We leave the second-floor shutters for the next day, when our friend, Don, is going to come over and help. My husband's just three months out from knee surgery replacement and he's got no business on a ladder.

We're starting to get and read reports that Maria is strengthening and she's moving closer to us. After Irma, its inconceivable for me to believe we were spared all of that to be hit ourselves. What was all the good work we did for St. Thomas and St. John if we're going to be hit ourselves?

I'm as anxious as the next person but I know anxiety isn't going to help or get things done. The usual list of locals on Facebook are already beating the panic button with fear, anxiety and a healthy dose of alarm. Where I can, I try to calm people I know or at least tamp down the hysteria.

Tuesday

I've gone to the sources that I trust. The ones that are not fear-mongering and are putting out facts. Maria has spun into a tight but angry hurricane. She has gained strength and she's going to be a Cat 4 or 5 coming within 10-30 miles of our south shore depending on which weather report you believe. The south shore is good for us personally. Our house faces the sea north and east. A south positioned storm will have to come over a mountain to get to us.

My husband and I go through the last of the storm prep at the pool. Our friend, Don, shows up and he helps me get the second story shutters and then hangs around to chat. The three of us swap various stories we've heard. We come to an agreement that it's likely a south shore storm, but it may damage out west—the pier. I think of all my friends who have invested so much to bring life to Frederiksted. Some fortunes undoubtedly will rise and fall. Don tells us to be safe and my husband starts the car to take him home.

It's the middle of the afternoon and we've moved the vehicles around. My SUV that we've owned for less than a year, had the power steering go out that morning. An inconvenience, we both agree, but we'll deal with it after. It's been raining off and on and I decide to snuggle the SUV more into the stone wall that fronts our courtyard. With no power steering, I struggle to position it, but I want to protect it as best I can.

We've moved most of our important stuff down to the first-floor bedroom where we spent Irma. I've packed up the few family heirlooms and secure them, in what I perceive, will be safer places.

My next goal is to get our semi-feral inside Crucian Siamese cat to move into the bathroom attached to our bedroom. It seems like it should be an easy task but she'd old, cranky and likes me—but not very much. She tolerates me.

I lure her into the bathroom where her food is normally kept; bribing her with her favorite treats. Then I snatch her up before she can think about and race across the kitchen to the other bathroom. I gently shove her in and close the door. I race back and collect all her things—scratching post, food and water bowls, litter box and then, as best as possible, rearrange them in her "new bathroom". She looks annoyed and terrified, all at once.

While I take the dog out for one last pee, for what may be a while; I catch, out of the corner of my eye, my husband fixing a cocktail. I get an early preview of his coping mechanism for the day.

I'm wired. It is impossible to describe the range of emotions you go through at this moment in time. I had a hard time catching my breath. My heart seems unnaturally fast. Think of preparing for something you dread and multiple times 10 and you may come close. I had lots of people ask me later why we didn't just leave. There were several factors. First, after Irma, we really believed that it just couldn't be another major storm. In other words, we thought we'd be ok. Also, by the time it became apparent that it was going to be bad; the airport was closed. Unlike hurricanes on the mainland; you can't just pick up and drive to another state.

It's 6:00 pm and starting to get dark. The wind has picked up and I think she'd going to come early. I read the last report of the night that says she's going to be 15-20 miles off the south shore. Someone has told me that a hurricane hunter said they were going to downgrade her to a 2. I ask the question of Facebook--has anyone else hear this? I instantly regret it. Two responses that were meaningless.

The power goes out.

My husband dutifully goes out and turns on the generator. Unlike Irma, two weeks earlier, the computer and cell phone do not come back on. We're on our own now.

The last we'd heard; Maria is supposed to come closest to St. Croix between 1-3 am. I hate nighttime storms. I have ever since I was a child in the Midwest where it wasn't hurricanes but tornadoes that scared the b'Jesus out of me.

By 7:30 pm the winds and rain have begun. Because of the way our house is tucked back into the mountain, even during Irma, we were able to open our front door and go outside. It's the closest to the generator and somewhat protected. My husband decides to go turn it off. While we don't know it for sure, it feels like it's getting rougher out.

It's almost immediate.

The winds sound like what I imagine it sounds like inside a wind tunnel.

It sounds cranked up.

We can feel the winds increasing.

The rains have really started coming and we make a gallows' humor joke about "at least the pool and the cistern will be full".

Besides our necessities, our room is filled with a variety of over-sized pillows—an order for one of my customers. I'm determined that they're one of the things that will survive Maria.

How do we solve a problem like Maria?

It's 10:00 pm.

The house is shaking, and I can see the pictures on the walls flapping. We never got this during Irma.

When people describe hurricanes sounding like a freight train that's not entirely accurate. They sound more like a really fast roller coaster—at least Maria did. We could hear her barreling down the side of the mountain toward our house and then it was as if the side of our house was the ramp up. She'd race up the side of our house and I'd hold my breath to see if she'd take the roof. This went on and on and on.

By now, my husband, is drunk and despite the valium I've taken, I'm stupidly anxious. I just want it to be over. Now.

I get up to check on the dog and realize there's water on the floor. A quick sniff confirms it's not him. I grab the flashlight and see a skim of water by the bedroom door. I grab the plastic bag of my customer's pillows and relocate them to higher ground before the water can get to them. I shake my sleeping husband. I really don't want him sleeping anyway. There is a reason that there is an expression that says, "misery loves company".

There's water on the floor."

He takes the flashlight from my hand and goes to the side door.

"It's not coming in from the outside door," he announces.

Great, I think. Then where is it coming from?

This bedroom sits directly over our cistern. I'm convinced, with the power out, the overflow pump is not working, and the water is rising from below, through the floor. My husband assures me that is mechanically impossible. I'm not convinced. I think my theory is right.

Maria is now screaming at us. I feel the pressure in my ears with each mad sweep. We are sweating profusely. The air is clogged and thick and makes breathing, already difficult from tension, more difficult. The dog, who is now on my sweaty lap is shaking uncontrollably.

My husband can't go back to sleep, despite the alcohol, because it is now stifling hot.

I make him start talking to me or at least listening to me.

"What was your happiest memory?"

This is one of those parlor games you play when you first start dating. But, if we've done it, I don't remember.

The birth of his children. Turning out in the trade.

I listen to the house shudder.

Roof, please hold on.

It calms.

My turn.

Graduating from college. Marrying him.

"I'm going to pay for not having that on my list, aren't I?" He mumbles.

"Not really," I say, and I mean it. I know how much he loves me. It's not a contest.

Another swell hits and I hear things snapping and flying. I hear a thump.

I know better than to ask what that was. Neither of us would know that.

She sounds and feels like she's slowing. My ears are popping less. I've sweated so much, my tee shirt is stuck to my chest and even though I haven't, my shorts are so wet it feels like I've peed my pants.

The swells are slowing down.

Finally, it feels like she's done. Whatever redecorating she was going to do; she's done. It's about 4:00 a.m.

"I'm going to go turn the generator on, if it's still there," he says as he trudges off.

He comes back.

The dog is sleeping.

I check on the cat who now owns the sink in the bathroom. There is still water on the floor, and I throw towels down to mop it up.

My husband is passed out on the bed. I lift the sticky sheets and curl in next to him. Exhausted.

We survived.

We fall into a deep sleep.

The Day after

We've been asleep what felt like 15 minutes but, in fact, was 2 ½ hours when we wake to voices calling our names. Our 'island children' trudged up the road to our house. As we stumble out of our sleep with cries of "we're here, we're here" and pull clothes on our naked, sweaty bodies; we stumble to the door. I can see the concern and relief laced on both of their faces.

"We're fine," I pronounce as we come out of the house squinting. Its foggy, steamy and looks like it wants to rain again.

We chat amiably with the kids. They depart assured that we're ok.

I start walking around to assess the damage.

> Security light-gone
>
> Two 80-foot trees—down
>
> Numerous hurricane shutters—gone
>
> Leaves ripped from every. Single. Plant.
>
> Boards yanked from the deck
>
> Gate-ripped from its hinges.

The list goes on.

The second layer of decking around our house looks like a bad game of pick up sticks—boards strewn everywhere.

Our Papaya trees—gentle creatures that they are—most are down.

Our amazing key lime tree has been ripped from its roots.

Guttering is tossed everywhere and our pool—with two trees in it—is already an unhealthy shade of green.

Despite everything, I fall to my knees in gratitude. I've no idea what others have been through, but I can surmise that we are lucky.

Generators and the Fine Art of Auto Mechanics

First, let me tell you, if you don't already know; generators are not made to run constantly. They are designed to fill in when your primary source of power gives out. Being married to an electrician gives me certain advantages that not every household has. My husband had wired the generator that came with out house so we could have 'complete power' when it was running. Some people were forced to run their generators just for their refrigerators or whatever major appliance they chose. We knew we could run our air conditioner, refrigerator, washer, (but not the dryer) and other small appliances. We didn't need to be concerned about the televisions because the service wouldn't be running for, probably, months after the power was restored.

A week after the storm, our neighbors, who had lost their roof had moved in with us; along with their two elderly dogs. We fell into a bit of a daily routine. At the top of that list had been to find propane that kept the generator running.

Propane generators were the norm and not the exception on our island; which meant that getting propane was a premium for lots of people.

For more than a week after the hurricane we were under a four-hour curfew, which meant from 12-4, roughly 50,000 people had four hours to do all their chores; which primarily consisted of survival. There were two propane companies that we had used in the past. It was my job to go to both and determine who could fill up our tanks the quickest. This was, unbeknownst to me at the time, a laughable proposition.

By the time I showed up at the first propane business, the line had snaked around the building and people were huddled as much in the shade as can be found in a 15" overhang. I walked to the back of the line and asked the first person I saw.

"Any propane available?"

The person stared at me like I had three heads.

"No one has come to the window yet," he said squinting at the sun.

"How long have you been waiting?" I asked somewhat perplexed.

"About an hour," came the calm response.

The man didn't seem stupid, but I couldn't get my head around standing in a line with new idea when someone would show up or if they would even show up. Fortunately, the other propane supplier was just a few steps away.

I walked away and felt the stares burning a hole in my back as if they knew something I didn't. I would come to realize that this was a common feeling for lots of us as we navigated it all.

The next business had fewer cars in the parking lot and more people seemed to be moving more efficiently. As I walked up to this line, I saw lots of people with cell phones plastered to their ears. When there was finally one who put their phone down, I asked what I thought was again a simple question.

"Are they delivering gas?"

The older gentleman looked at me and shook his head.

"Have you ordered already."

"No", I answered honestly.

"Ma'am they won't have more propane besides existing orders for a while."

I stared at him incredulously. How is that possible, I was asking myself. Everyone on this island needs propane. I must have looked flustered or lost or something. He reached out and patted my arm.

"It usually gets delivered faster than what they say."

I started shuffling back to the car. This was my one task for the day, and I had failed. How had that happened? I wasn't sure what I was supposed to do or say and there was literally no place else to go. We had a bit more remaining and if we needed to, we could use the tank attached to our stove but that was a court of last resort.

I tried to process what could be my next alternative and through my caffeine/vodka addled mind; I could come up with nothing. Literally nothing.

I made my way home and as I turned the corner to go up the hill; out of the corner of my eye, I spied a propane truck making its way up the hill to our neighbors. Honestly there was no logic in my reasoning, but I turned as fast as I could and chased the truck up the hill.

I don't think this was the first time this had happened to this driver.

"Hey," I said clamoring out of my car and pushing my sweaty hair back off my face and trying not to look as desperate as I felt. "Do you have any propane you could deliver to our house?"

It was obvious to me that I wasn't the first desperate person to chase him down.

"Not today," he said matter-of-factly as he continued to fill up his customer's tank. "Where you live?" He asked jerking his head to the street.

I decided to downplay my desperation and try for sweet ingénue—no matter how pathetic it would look.

"Just down the road," I tried batting my sweaty eyelashes and unsticking my wet tee shirt. Just as I thought I was making some progress; as I said, I was somewhat delusional—a woman eased herself out of the passenger side of the truck and with a sideways glance that would lay flat anyone, looked me up and down as if to say—forget it sweetie, this ain't happening.

On the best of days, my flirting skills suck and this was decidedly not one of my best days.

"Look," I said eyeing them both. I decided honesty was the best policy at this point. "I've got four people living in my house. Most of us haven't showered in a while because we've been trying to get supplies. If you can just get us some propane today—and we'll pay you cash—I promise to go and put in a proper order and get at the back of the line just like everyone else. Please."

I am not sure if it was the desperation in my voice and just the realization that I wasn't going to leave easily; whatever, he shook his head and said,

"Wait here."

And so, I did.

I've heard stories about liquid gold strikes in the early days of the rush in Colorado and how it becomes an addiction when you find it. I'm not sure if it is a fair comparison but that day it was to me. Hot, sweaty, exhausted and smelly; I carried with me a sense of pride as the propane truck made its way up to our house and to our propane tank. I think Napoléon must have had just the same sense of satisfaction that I did that day. Yup, I'm just sure of it.

Coke Addiction (and I'm not talking about the white stuff)

Any health care professional will tell you that soft drinks are bad for you. I mean bad for you. Have you ever seen someone use a soft drink to get corrosion off a car motor? I promise you; you will never look at that can of soda, the same way, ever again.

While I was in college, I drank a lot of "real" Coke. And I drank it by the liter. There was a small issue with me ballooning into a larger size my senior year of college; but that's another story.

As we continued to work through our post-hurricane status, we had come to the realization that we were drinking just a bit too much alcohol. Think a large bottle of vodka a night and you get the picture. Initially it was a coping mechanism but as time wore on; it became a habit. And, no question about it, it was a bad habit. Much as what happened when I quit smoking years ago; my desire to cut back on alcohol was replaced by something else—Coke.

With decades of Coke jingles ringing in my ears, I began it somewhat innocently. I'd have a Coke for lunch and that would be it. I started adding a Coke in the afternoon to give me my caffeine jolt. Soon enough, this was joined by an evening Coke (well ahead of 7:00 p.m. so as not to interfere with my sleep). I honestly didn't see it as particularly bad since it was replacing an even worse habit. My PA had a different view of it.

Her: How much Coke are you drinking a day?

Me: Not much, one, two glasses.

Her: How many ounces?

Me: Um, 10, 12 ok 16.

Her: Do those two glasses include refills?

Me: Damn, how do you know that?

Her: Your weight is going up. Think there's a connection?

Me: Absolutely not.

Her: Let's take a break and see where that goes.

Me: It is literally the only vice I have these days.

Her: Let's just try.

Me: (heavy sigh) Is there no other alternative? What if I gave up coffee?

Her: This isn't a negotiation.

Me: I hate logic.

Her: So that's a yes?

Me: (thinking expletives) Alright fine.

I could tell you that this was an instantaneous change; but that would be a lie and I'm certain, somewhere down the line my PA would rat me out. I approached it like anyone would who is being told to do something for their own well-being. Especially, if that someone is a 15-year-old. Because that is precisely how I behaved. In my defense, dropping Coke gave me monstrous headaches (don't tell me it's not addictive) and I was just not pleasant to be around. So, I eased into it. I cut down to 1 a day and then 4 a week and eventually I went off it and I'll be damned if she wasn't right. My weight did go down and I started feeling better.

It is safe to say, that you will, from time to time, see me with a Coke in my hand. Like any bad habit, it does still creep back occasionally. I try not to let it define me or upset me too much. I get back on the wagon and stop. And really, truly, you don't have to believe me that it's bad for you. Just go pour a can over something rusty and see for yourself.

Hometown Heroes (Tim Duncan, I'm looking at you)

One of things that I have learned; having gone through a hurricane is being a big island (think Puerto Rico) or constantly on the news (think Florida) gets you lots of attention and that attention will eventually get you some outside relief you weren't expecting. From politicians to celebrities, everyone wants to look like they're helping. And some do.

I don't know Tim Duncan personally. When we moved to St. Croix, it was hard not to get to know him. Famous basketball player done good with the San Antonio Spurs. He was born and raised on our small island and the pride he brings out in locals is infectious. The advertising of one of his endorsements is just a boy from St. Croix.

I did some homework on him after we'd lived here a while just to see if I could find out anything more about him. He played his whole career with the San Antonio Spurs. That, in and of itself, is a feat when you consider how often major sports athletes move around or, in fairness, get traded. Not him. He loved San Antonio and apparently the feeling was mutual. He is considered one of the greatest power forwards of all time (no slouch is he). He is a five-time NBA champion, two-time NBA MVP, three-time NBA Finals MVP and an NBA All-Star game MVP. So sayeth Wikipedia. His 6'11" frame played for Wake Forest in college (they retired his number) and he was a first-round draft pick. He also played for the USA Olympic team in 2004. Most people on the island know the story of young Tim. He was a swimmer and only took up basketball after Hurricane Hugo destroyed the only Olympic size pool on the island. So, at what is considered a ripe age of 14, he took up basketball.

Now, unless you're a basketball freak (or you live on St. Croix or in San Antonio), I'm guessing you don't know much about Tim Duncan—despite these impressive stats. Why? Well, if I had to identify one thing, I would say it is that Tim Duncan, doesn't like the spotlight. He is good at his sport and he doesn't seek publicity. I'm sure you can think of a few athletes that fall into that "publicity seeking" category. Tim Duncan is consistently referred to as one of the "good guys". So why am I talking about him here?

First, you need to understand that Tim Duncan has never forgotten his experience during Hurricane Hugo, a monster storm that crippled the island and essentially changed the trajectory of his life and career. Because he hasn't sought the spotlight, it was somewhat surprising for a lot of people that he penned an Op-ed entitled "To my friends, family and all U.S. Virgin Islanders: I'm not giving up on you". It was an honest, candid piece on how Hugo had affected him and how the Virgin Islands were being ignored following Irma and Maria. As he so aptly put "Puerto Rico may get all the attention regarding Maria's destruction. But before the immense storm wreaked havoc there, it sent tornado-like winds on a direct line across St. Croix." See, Tim Duncan understood that even though Maria was 10 miles off our shore; with a 7-mile-wide island; it's as if it hit us directly.

I don't ever want to get into a tit-for-tat discussion about who is more deserving or whom was devastated more. In hurricanes, there are no winners, only losers. What I can tell you is that once Maria hit Puerto Rico; St. Croix and the rest of the Virgin Islands fell off the radar screen. I know because my mainland family and friends were desperate for information in the immediate days after and all they could find was about Puerto Rico.

Tim Duncan decided this simply wasn't acceptable. In his retirement, he could have simply written a check and let someone else do the heavy lifting. But, apparently, that is not how Tim Duncan is wired. Out of the gate, he did write a check for $250,000. His Op-ed followed shortly thereafter. He set a goal of $5 million dollars for medical supplies, food, etc. He personally matched $1 million that was raised. He sent planes loaded with supplies within days after the hurricane. And then he sent another and another. Oh, and he was on every single plane. He's been modest about what he has done but it is safe to say that many people would not have survived had he not stepped up and provided the relief that he did.

I'd also be remiss if I didn't mention country singer Kenny Chesney. Chesney, who calls St. John his second home was also an all-star in hurricane relief for St. Thomas and St. John that were almost leveled by Hurricane Irma. Again, in a very unassuming way, he brought supplies to those islands that were then further damaged by Hurricane Maria 10 days later. Friends from St. John said he would show up at pub and just sing for whatever size of crowd happen to be there. Here's a man who draws thousands to stadium size concerts playing for some hurricane weary neighbors—not because he must or is looking for attention—but because it's his gift and he is generous to share it.

Both men gave tirelessly and freely and continue to do so.

Tim Duncan tells a story of living on Chef Boy-r-dee following Hugo. I can certainly relate to that. For weeks following the hurricane, fresh produce was at a premium and scarce. Our local farmers had lost all their crops so everything we got fresh had to be imported. We were well stocked with canned chicken and tuna, cans of spaghetti and ravioli. You develop somewhat of a numbness in your taste buds when you are relegated, for a long period, to canned food. Tim Duncan has never forgotten that experience he went through at such a young age.

My most enduring memory of Tim Duncan will be the distribution he made for Thanksgiving dinner. He had assembled a line of volunteers and arrived with all the foods important for a proper Thanksgiving dinner. Then, in the blaze of a hot and humid November day, he stood there with the rest of the volunteers. He did it not because he had to do it but because he wanted to do it. This 6'11" giant of a man in both body and heart handed out food to his fellow Crucians with a smile and a handshake. You see there is a big difference between just writing a check and writing a check with your soul. For the people of the Virgin Islands; we were lucky that Tim Duncan did both.

And while his fundraising work continues; he has blended back into his quiet life that he had before he thrust himself back in the spotlight for an island that will always be home to him. He will always have a seat at the table at any home on St. Croix.

Thanks Tim Duncan. You're my hero.

The Politics of Hurricanes and Paper Towels

By now, most of you know that hurricanes, I don't care where they happen, are a disruptive event. There's no getting around that. Think Hurricane Sandy, Hurricane Katrina, etc. What you find with hurricanes is that they bring out the best and the worst in people (see my chapter on Tim Duncan). Politicians are a mixed bag. I can say that since I'm a recovering one, but that's a different book.

Here's what generally happens after a hurricane occurs. First the National Guard usually makes an appearance. We were very happy about that. Then the relief agencies and their workers show up (that's a complex issue). Then, usually sprinkled in there are the politicians. Some good. Some bad.

Our Governor held daily press conferences to catch us up on what was happening in the territory during the recovery period. There's only one problem. He was broadcasting them to people who didn't have power. I heard, several months later, that people who had found out about it; had listened to it in their cars. But, here's the thing. How was anyone supposed to know about it? The paper wasn't being published (no power). The radio stations were barely working (again, a power thing). How in the WORLD were you suppose to listen to something you didn't know existed? It was months later, and I'm not kidding it was months, before I had even heard they'd happened. A good friend of mine told me over lunch one day that she and her husband had gone out to their car every day and listened to the daily briefings. Terribly inventive but let's be honest, bizarre. And before you ask about those crank radios that are supposed to be so awesome for people without power—don't. They don't work and for the most part; they were nonexistent on St. Croix.

The Puerto Rican Governor was a bit more unusual. He had problems getting things done because his folks were annoyed at the relief workers who were coming down and taking "their jobs". Honestly, who CARES after a hurricane? Isn't this about getting people back to normal as quickly and as safely as humanly possible? We heard stories of equipment sitting at the airport because the local workers were blocking access. I have no idea if it was legitimately true but if it was; shame on them.

What you probably heard the most about from Puerto Rico was the back and forth between the Mayor of San Juan and the President of the United States. That's an interesting juxtaposition of two people, who, you would think, would be able to find common ground during a crisis. But you would be wrong.

It started when the President came to Puerto Rico to check on relief efforts. Most people that know me, know I don't have much use for this President for a whole litany of reasons but his visit to PR really moved to the top of the list.

After surveying some of the massive damage that the island took; he did, what I am sure he thought was a savvy (and probably generous) act. He threw rolls of paper towels at residents.

To do what? Wipe up water? Clean their bathrooms? Soak up their tears? I am not sure what aide told him it was a good idea but I'm assuming they're no longer employed. The photo op alone was catastrophic. But let's be honest; what could any human being genuinely do with all this misery and suffering around them. The smart ones work on ways to cut that misery and suffering down quickly. They usually do a lot behind the scenes—declare states of emergency, access necessary funds, send troops if necessary. The ability of politicians to mobilize resources in a meaningful way is endless. When I saw the video of him throwing paper towels at these hapless beings; I'm not sure what I thought but stunned was the first thing that came to mind. It also reminded me of the expression my mother used so much when we were growing up—if you don't have anything nice to say, then don't say anything at all. If your first reaction to human suffering is a bad one (and you should recognize that) then just don't make one—please.

But lest you think its just national politicians who are tone deaf—I give you our legislature.

During the recovery period when most citizens did not have power; our elected officials, ALL OF THEM, went to Washington, DC to appear before Congress and ask for money. I do not, in any way begrudge them the necessity of the trip but really ALL OF THEM? You can somewhat excuse Donald Trump. He's not the smartest bulb and he doesn't live here. But THEY DO. So, while their constituents were without power; without running water; without basic services; they were staying in air conditioned, nice hotels with every creature comfort their citizens did not have. Talk about tone deaf. AND to add insult to injury; we paid for it. It was honestly one of the most blatant use of excess I've seen from elected officials in a very long time and I've been around politics for 25 years. Did they apologize? No. Did they equivocate? Oh, you betcha.

So, to recap. If you're going to be an elected official and you really want to serve your citizens well and you have the misfortune of being one during a catastrophe, natural or otherwise—no throwing paper towels at anyone and no taking boondoggles. Actually, it really doesn't matter if something bad is happening. Just don't do either of these things.

B&B or Hurricane Refugee Center

One of the things that happened within days of the hurricane was some neighbors moving in with us. They had lost their roof (yes, they were some of the unfortunate souls) and they had been staying at another neighbor's house who had opened their home to lots of people. But, as can happen, their generator broke and everyone had to move out. My husband happened to be there when the announcement came down and without a moment's hesitation he said, "you're moving in with us". I've had a lot of people ask me if I was bothered that he volunteered without asking me and the answer is absolutely not. There was so much misery and grief following Maria that if you were lucky enough to still have a roof (and we were lucky enough) then you did everything you possibly could to mitigate anyone else's suffering. This was our way to mitigate and candidly if I'd been there, I would have done the same thing.

Jennie and Hop were a perfectly lovely couple that we barely knew. We would pass them on morning walks with our dog, Huck and their two senior citizen dogs, Stella and Junior. We weren't entirely sure how Huck would handle roommates, but he showed us the way by a smile and a wag of his tail.

While we didn't know how long they would be staying (not knowing what the insurance company was going to do and all); we did know that they had a long-awaited trip to Portugal in a few months and they would be with us until then.

It is an astonishing thing, in hindsight, to see what a well-oiled machine the four of us became. Because the first several weeks were built around survival; we all left each day with assignments. They took on getting ice for the cooler because the refrigerator broke (another chapter) and Frank and I took on generator maintenance and propane. Well he took on generator maintenance and I took on the propane search. Each night we would regroup to talk about the day's events around amazing home cooked meals that one of us prepared. Hop got Frank to try turnips and beets roasted on the grill and Frank would make some ridiculously good grilled meat. Jennie and I usually whipped up the side dishes and made sure that there was plenty of wine or Rum or Vodka—whatever the night called for.

Outside of college, I'd never really lived with someone I didn't know. I'd gone from home to college and then lived for a while by myself before getting married. So, living with grown-ups, I wasn't related to, for an unknown period was something new. I can tell you at the time, I didn't think it was strange at all. Which in and of itself is strange, but there you go.

Junior (on the left) and Huck chilling after their morning walk.

We battled black flies and exploding generators (again another chapter) and the rush to use food before it spoiled and wayward rats. We figured out how to get our dogs to play together nicely and keep my dog from eating all their dog's special food. We cooked together and cleaned together and laughed together and shared stories.

And here's the thing. We lived with these folks for not quite two months and during that time, we didn't have one single cross word. Not one. One of the by products of not having access to technology in your house—which we didn't for four months—is it forces you to do other things. So, we talked to each other. We talked to each other a lot and learned about each other's lives. Hop had great stories to share of St. Croix in another time and his experiences after Hugo. Jennie has the most **OMG** story about her trips to Jamaica. These are things you don't learn about people; even when you're living down the street from one another. You just don't have that kind of space with people. But, in a home where, in the evenings your activities were limited; you revert to what really connects people. Conversation.

For four days one week after our original generator broke but before the new one was on island—we had no power. None. We had a propane stove and of course, the gas grill but when it got dark, we had to rely on my cadre of candles. Lucky for everyone I'm a candle freak. I've told this story a million times and I always get disbelieving looks but I swear it's true. Those were four of my favorite days of my life. I kid you not. Telling stories and cooking and eating and laughing by candlelight is about as intimate as you can get with other people around a table. Hop using my oven mitts as castanets, before bringing food in off the grill. None of us really wanted to go to our hot rooms with no light and face a misery of sleeping in the heat. So, we lingered at the table and lit more candles and we never ran out of things to talk about.

I've used this line about Jennie and Hop many times, but it is a fact. Solitude (where we live) made us neighbors but Maria made us friends.

The time passed quickly and soon they had packed up to head out for their trip. Our other neighbor (where they'd originally stayed) had fixed their generator and Hop and Jennie were moving into one of their apartments when they returned. It made sense because we all knew their time with us wasn't forever. We said our goodbyes and told them to have a great time on their trip.

Several days passed and I get a text message from my friend, Rene. She and her husband had escaped to California to family right after the hurricane because of work demands. They were returning and leaving the villa they'd been in, to move into a friend's cottage. Only one problem. The cottage wouldn't be ready in time for their booked return tickets. The conversation went something like this.

Rene: Hey honey how's it going?

Me: Good and you?

Rene: Good, we've got our tickets booked to come home but there is a glitch. The cottage won't be ready for us for a couple of days. I know I told you we wouldn't need a place to stay, but….

Me: Of course, you can stay with us, don't even give it a thought.

Rene: I promise it will only be for a few days.

Me: Honestly, it's ok. The room is clean, so you're all set.

Rene: Thanks so much.

I sat the phone down after the texting and just smiled. The thing about a small island is, it really is a small town made up of people you care about and some you don't know and others you live with from time to time. Post hurricane is generally a popular time to get to know your neighbors and even live with them for a while.

"Oh Frank, Rene and Jay are going to stay with us for a few days when they get back on island. Is that ok?"

And without missing a beat…

"Of course, it is. You didn't even need to ask!"

"I know dear, but I just thought I would".

Electrical Wires, Sink Holes and Crappy Roads

If you've been to the Caribbean, really any part of the Caribbean then you know that we have really, really, really, crappy roads. The road my husband and I live on hasn't been paved since it was turned into a paved road from gravel roughly 20 years ago. It is something you don't necessarily like it, but you put up with it. As we say about many things; it's the price we pay for living in paradise.

Immediately following the hurricane, the island was on curfew and then when the National Guard arrived; we were not only on curfew, but we started being redirected from roads so that they could begin cleaning up. All were completely legitimate reasons to redirect traffic. There's just one problem. Most ways in and out of both cities generally pass through very specific roads. But let's start with the initial problem.

On an island where virtually every telephone and electrical line has been taken down; the first few days after the storm became a bit of a dodging game. Dodging poles. Dodging electrical wires. Dodging debris from homes. Dodging trees. You get the picture. Most people were good at getting out and dislodging or moving whatever obstruction was in the road. The problem with that, of course, is that it then slows down traffic. The National Guard did what they could, but our electrical grid is old and many of the poles and lines were equally antiquated. Most of the debris was cleaned up and the wires pushed to the side. For the most part...

Once the curfew hours were shortened, we were able to be out at dusk and not have the need to fight all the traffic earlier in the day. But then the sinkhole happened.

Where my husband and I live is on the east end of the island. There are two ways to get to where we live from Christiansted; but one, is oh so much shorter. A couple of weeks after the hurricane, two sinkholes began to develop at a part of the East End loop. One cratered the road and was literally closed within 24 hours. This wasn't just a little inconvenience; it was a major inconvenience. Because, even though there was another road, it was now significantly longer because it was on the south shore road where the hurricane hit the hardest and so, the debris was not only more, it was worse. There were parts where you had to duck electrical poles that were handing across the road and wires that had been tied back by either National Guard or concerned citizens. To say it was dangerous, is an understatement. There was no way to gauge the integrity of anything that was being held back. None.

So now we have one road we can't use because of a sinkhole and another road that you can use but is made dangerously impassable by the wires and poles and trash everywhere. But, as you have no doubt surmised, we had to go on a daily basis for ice and other essentials.

My husband and I set out for what we knew was going to be a somewhat arduous trip. We got through the first mile or so relatively unscathed. But then came the bit dodgier parts of the road. The pavement is actually amazing on this stretch of road. Much more so than almost any other place on the island. So, while we had to watch for lines and debris; we didn't have to worry about potholes.

I got out twice to move limbs from the road (apparently still blowing around even after the storm) and more than once to tie up a line that had come undone. The good news was we didn't have to worry about hot wires (no power and all that) so at least that step was ok.

This was our daily navigation for four days while they worked to repair the sinkhole.

One day, while coming home at dusk; we both missed a series of wires that had moved into the road. With absolutely no time to react; the wires acted like they were alive and whipped around our side rearview mirror, across the glass and finally stopping when my husband stopped the car. To say our hearts stopped; wouldn't describe it. We both got out and made sure that the tire hadn't been affected and stared at the etching the wires had left on both the car window and the side door and the rear-view mirror. It wasn't pretty but nothing was broken so we got back into our newly scarred car and drove home.

The next day the sink hole had been repaired. Honestly, most of us were shocked at the speed of the repair and I think we all had anticipated a longer time. The second sink hole didn't present nearly the danger and it moved to the "don't worry about it" list for both us and the road crews. In fact, it was MONTHS after the hurricane before anything was done about it. But remember, I told you, our road hasn't been repaired since it was paved. So, there's that.

Power

At 8:50 on December 15, 2017, 88 days after Maria took our power away; this handsome, God-like lineman restored our power. I fell to my knees and wept.

Hurricane Sex

You probably didn't see this chapter coming or maybe you did. Either way, here we go. I'm sure there are members of my family, including my husband who will be horrified that I'm discussing this; but I promise, they'll get over it!

When you're in the initial throws of survival after a catastrophic event; pretty much everything that is and has been normal in your life goes out the window including, assuming you're having it—sex. It's not that you don't love your partner, or you don't want to be intimate; it's just that if you haven't showered in a few days and the heat is monstrous and the power doesn't work; well, let's just say your mind is elsewhere. But, like everything else; once you begin to develop a routine; you notice the things that have been missing and if you're lucky (and I am lucky) you want to get back to those good and pleasurable things.

So, as was bound to happen at some point; my husband and I wanted to have sex. Now, before you get all freaked out and think I'm going to describe it; relax. This isn't that kind of book. No, what I want you to picture is how to be intimate with neighbors living in your house and doors you can't really close because of the heat. Add to that windows you can't close and the constant hum of generators in the neighborhood (kind of a mood breaker) and you can see where "getting in the mood" is a challenge. But I was a Girl Scout growing up and I'm from the Midwest so I kind of like a challenge!

I can't honestly say that I had planned it all out but one day, I knew for a fact that our roommates were going to be gone part of the time during the 7-9 at night time when we ran the generator. This meant we could be running the air conditioner. That meant we could close the doors and windows and have some privacy and quiet.

Now let me preface by saying that my husband and I love each other very much. We fight, like every other couple on the planet and we've gone through rough patches but our genuine love for each other is strong. Sometimes, however, love does not translate into speed and knowing you are on a clock—tic toc—doesn't help with the mood.

But back to romance. So, the air conditioner was on. We had chilled cocktails. The dog, who wasn't missing out on the air conditioning, was slumbering in his bed. We had both showered and didn't smell and didn't have Sahara dust clinging to our clothes. I set my iPhone to some soft music and pulled down the freshly laundered sheets.

I must tell you something else that I PROMISE will embarrass my husband (if this chapter hasn't already) but he is a world class kisser. It's TRUE! If there were an Olympic sport in kissing, my husband would have multiple medals. Among many things, it is one of my favorite things about him. So, we were leisurely taking our time to get in the mood. We were kissing and laughing and generally exorcising our demons of the day. I could find myself relaxing and just melting into my husband's arms. While we were not in a hurry; we were both very conscious of the time.

Things were progressing (again, not that kind of a book) and we were, shall we say at a critical juncture in the evening; when, suddenly and without zero warning, the air-conditioning shut off. And by off, I mean, not the off when WAPA goes out but the off that someone had turned off the generator. Besides the fact that this is extremely hard on the air conditioner; it is a monumental mood killer because along with the cold air leaving, the music died, and it didn't take long for the closed windows and doors in the room to start making the room hot.

Frank was at a lost as to what would cause it but at the exact moment, he spoke those words out loud; I heard the front door open and close. Ah, roommates back early.

I sprang out of bed and threw on some clothes and opened the bedroom door to see my suspicions confirmed.

"Aw Hop, what happened to the generator?" I asked trying to sound normal.

"I turned it off," came the reply.

"Any particular reason for that," I said casually? "We were kind of in the middle of something."

"It was flaming."

I can assure you that the mood killer worse then the air-conditioner going off is hearing that the generator is on fire.

So, mood killed. Generator on fire. Clothes back on.

As my husband climbed out of bed to go slay the dragon; he looked over his shoulder at me wistfully and said, "tomorrow?"

"Yes," I smiled at him. "Tomorrow, my love."

Refrigerators and Why You Don't Need Them (Just kidding)

By day 9 of the hurricane, our 17-year-old refrigerator started to show its age. With the electricity at our house only on 6 hours a day; we knew it wouldn't last much longer. By week two, we had stopped using the refrigerator side of the refrigerator and now we're using the freezer for that. It's just a matter of time...

The next day, I saw an ant trail going into the refrigerator. I tell my husband and he just shrugs at me. I am really getting tired of people shrugging at me.

Surprisingly, it wasn't the refrigerator that died first but our generator. And then, when we got the new generator, the refrigerator finally died. The ant trail was a sign of its demise, so no one is surprised.

Hop and Jennie are continuing their daily quests for ice. Now that is not only important; it is necessary.

My husband has hauled out a garage sale find from the previous summer—an old but large cooler. It assumes its place alongside our refrigerator. I think we're trying to make it grow up to be a refrigerator and use our dead refrigerator as its role model.

We emptied everything into it that absolutely, positively needs to stay refrigerated and put everything in every cabinet that can hold it. Since Hop is such an amazing cook; he had moved in with a variety of herbs and vegetables and all types of culinary magic and we must find the proper place for it.

It becomes apparent, quickly, that milk, in ice, in an old cooler will barely last two days. So, the immediate is to buy smaller bottles to avoid throwing out spoiled milk. It also is readily evident that you better know what is exactly in the jars, because, once the ice starts turning to water; it will, if not the first day, but the second, lose its label. And suddenly your dinner "surprise" is either pickle relish or green salsa. You're never exactly sure.

The other thing, I'm sure you've never given much thought to is how your refrigerator is laid out. When you are first shopping for your refrigerator, you pay attention to shelving—place for eggs, butter, vegetables and fruit, etc. As refrigerators have progressed, they have become more and more sophisticated. Soon, they'll be shopping for us! Well, one can only hope. But here's the thing. Most coolers do not have shelves. Oh, some of the hi-tech ones may have small pieces you can put in to simulate shelves but even those don't work when the ice starts melting. I think you see where this is going. You have no way to organize either by item or age. And once the ice starts melting and it turns into water and you lose the labels—well then, you're really screwed. I remember many mornings, putting my hand in the freezing ice to find the apple I put in there yesterday; only to find the tomato that was purchased last week, and we forgot about.

And here is something you don't have to do with refrigerators—clean them out once a week! Because of the above example I gave you; it was not unheard of to find a lost and forgotten peach at the bottom of the cooler. It did have a spigot on it and about every other day we would drag in to the edge of the steps in our entry way and drain off the water. So, it wasn't like we didn't try. But, inevitably, something would float to the top after a few weeks and we would all look at each other like, 'got any idea what that is'? The answer was generally no.

This went on for quite some time and despite our best efforts; we never could quite master this. When I look back on what we had to do that bothered me the most; this was at the top of the list. Lots of people talk about the fun indoor camping can be. I can assure that when you MUST do indoor camping; there is nothing fun about it. In many ways, it was the constant reminder of our situation and our inability to fix it on our own.

We did absolutely nothing about replacing it for a new refrigerator until our power was entirely connected. And then, we were told to wait a few days to connect anything, in case all the bugs hadn't been worked out.

All told, we lost two refrigerators (we had a small one in our bedroom), my electric toothbrush, two computers, a coffee maker and a clock. The constant on and off of the generator and probably also their age contributed to their death.

Once it felt like an 'all clear' had been given to us; we drove straight to the Kmart/Sears appliance store in Sunny Isle shopping center. We walked through the rows of shiny refrigerators and stared at them like lovers. My husband pulled my arms back twice as I moved into hug one. A bit much, he muttered to me.

At last we started to linger in front of a few of our favorites and the sales clerk, apparently now convinced that we were serious ambled over to talk with us.

My husband asked just two questions.

1. Is the price negotiable?
2. Can it be delivered tomorrow?

We got a 'yes' answer to both questions and within 24 hours we were the proud owners of a stainless-steel Maytag Refrigerator. We just sat in our chairs and stared at it. One more step back to civilization.

Hurricane Diet

Ask anyone and they will tell you that your food options become somewhat limited after a hurricane either by lack of supplies or inability to prepare them properly.

As I said in the Tim Duncan chapter, in an interview after the hurricane, he said that when he went through Hugo; his family had subsisted on Chef-Boyardee. I think it was mostly spaghetti. Well, all I can say is 'I get it'.

Let me preface this by saying that all the hurricane prep guides say prepare ahead of the hurricane with 1-2 weeks of food. I had planned on 10 days—water, canned goods of all variety. So, I felt like we were ok. We also had $500 in cash which also seemed like a reasonable amount. Let me tell you why neither of those facts are true.

1. Because Maria was so catastrophic, grocery stores were limited in what they could initially get because of transportation issues. Canned goods? No issue. Fresh produce, meat, etc.? An issue.
2. $500 is a lot of money. But not only did it have to cover food; it had to cover gas and frankly any other incidentals. Why? Because the banks were not initially opened after the storm and even when they did; not all the ATMs were working. Factor in, with no power, stores couldn't run their credit card machines and you can see where $500 can disappear quick.

I think I mentioned, at one point, that hurricanes bring out the best and the worst in people. Let me share with you a best.

Expressway Market is a small mom and pop store run by two cousins. As a matter of fact, they had only owned it a few months when Maria landed. These are young men with families and busy lives of their own; who always greeted you with a hello and a smile.

Once we ran out of money and that just took a few days; we were down to our squirreled away money which wasn't much. Because the other bigger grocery store had a line out the door for ice; we decided to go to Expressway Mart for some essentials—essentials that were leaving the shelves quickly. I picked up what produce I could find, some canned goods and the real necessities—two bottles of vodka. Don't judge, we could only go out of the house four hours a day. I estimated my costs and waited in line. The owners were hot, tired and like the rest of us, trying to make do. With no power they had to use a hand calculator and some very dim lights. Ever seen windows in a grocery store that open? Of course, you haven't because most don't have them. So here we all are; packed in tightly in a small building with dim lights and no air conditioning. Whole Foods, it was not. I finally make my way to the front of the line and he adds up my groceries. Despite the fact, that I'm an ex-banker, I was way off. I promptly pick up the vodka bottles, while grimacing, I set them aside. He subtracts those and I'm still short. Shit, I mumble. The people behind me are starting to fidget and I stare at the items in front of me as if one of them will magically remove itself from the counter. I must have looked shell-shocked and what seemed like an eternity, I'm sure was only seconds. Suddenly, I feel a hand on mine and I look up to see him smiling at me.

"It's just food," he said, "take it."

"I promise to pay it back," I said, and I meant it.

You see. Sometimes people really do listen to their better angels.

After that first fiasco and with the oncoming termination of the refrigerator, I decide that we should focus on as much canned goods as possible and eureka, that became Chef-Boyardee.

When we were growing up, I didn't know that Chef-Boyardee wasn't particularly nutritious. I just knew that it had yummy spaghetti sauce and meatballs that you could pop in your mouth. I saw our return to these delicacies as a return to my youth. At least that's what I told myself. By the time the power came back on, months later, I wasn't even bothering to heat it up. The flower was off the bloom, as they say, and I'd just crack open a can and grab a fork. Honestly, it even disgusted my husband. Truly, if I never see a can of Chef-Boyardee again; I'll be fine. I even coast by them now in the grocery store. Too many memories.

The other food item that wore out its welcome was canned chicken and its fair cousin, tuna.

Once we were able to start communicating with the outside; everyone was asking us what we needed. And people, our friends and family, being the loving souls that they are, bought us everything that was on the list I published on Facebook. Which meant we didn't get 5 large cans of chicken; we got 20.

My husband said that when his kids were little, he used to hide the venison he brought home in lasagna and spaghetti. They never fell for it.

I'm not a bad cook myself and I fancied myself clever enough to fix the chicken a variety of ways. Which I did. At first, it worked. We had chicken casserole. We had chicken tetrazzini. But eventually I ran out of steam and just started making chicken salad.

"Is this tuna," my husband asked one day?

"No dear, it's chicken."

"We haven't run out of it yet?"

"Not by a long shot," I chuckled.

And truth to tell, we had cans left over even after the power was restored. It was several months later before I could bring myself to use what was left.

Eventually, the restaurants started reopening (although Blue Water Terrace and The Deep End were both open the next day) and we would go out occasionally to take a break from the canned goods and shooting for something green and leafy. We didn't do it a lot because getting around the island for several months was still a bit dicey.

All of this combined with the constant flow of alcohol did not help our waistlines and the pounds crept on quickly. I'd like to say we were bothered by it but that would be a lie. We had so many other pressing issues that gaining weight just didn't make the list. We knew, at some point, there would be a day of reckoning, but it wasn't today, and it probably wasn't next week. And again, I emphasize, we were some of the lucky ones. We had a generator and a way to cook the food we were able to purchase or was shipped to us. Some of my fellow citizens weren't so lucky and the MREs (meals ready to eat) that the National Guard had provided, became their primary sustenance for most of the days following the hurricane. And like a generator, I don't think a person is meant to eat those alone.

Like so many things that happened in those following days, I look back on them with a sense of amazement that we were able to figure it out. I won't be publishing a hurricane diet cookbook, but if I did, I guarantee you it wouldn't include canned chicken or, sorry Chef-Boyardee, Chef-Boyardee.

The USPS

As you might expect, getting things to the island after the hurricane was a bit of an issue.

One of the primary shipping companies was looted multiple times and then, for good measure, burned to the ground. FedEx and UPS were trying to get back up, but again with planes being an issue, it was slow. Interestingly, on my little island, the United States Postal Service has always been the most reliable carrier. We have more post offices per population than probably anywhere else in the world. Hyperbole? Maybe. But I'm sticking to it.

So, the USPS it was.

It was several days before they were able to open their doors and then, like every other business, they couldn't use their credit card processing machines. But what made their situation even more complicated was that their computers ran on a phone system that was down across the island. And, as you probably know, the USPS needs computers to process your mail. So, every day was a guessing game as to whether their system was up or down. To their credit, it wasn't the workers' fault and every day, they patiently waited to see if the system would work and deal with irritated, cranky islanders looking for care packages from the mainland. And lest we make the system TOO simple, they didn't just need the computer for the mail going out, but they needed it for the mail coming in. So, if the computer was down and EVEN IF your package had arrived, there was no guarantee you were going home with it.

Most of us walked in with an optimistic attitude that "today was the day" we'd be able to mail and receive. It took a bit of psyching up; but we tried.

Marjorie the postal employee who had the patience of a SAINT, would routinely and politely calm people down who were having nervous breakdowns waiting on packages. Most people understood it wasn't Marjorie's fault that the system wasn't working. But, as is often the case, she was the messenger. I just have to say this. I was in there multiple times to pick up packages. Time after time when the computers weren't working or the generator had stopped or they were out of supplies or all the above and not once, not one little time, did Marjorie lose her cool. I always liked Marjorie's dry sense of humor but after all of that, I admired her skills because that lady has skills.

One day, it was our turn. The packages we had been breathlessly waiting for from Michelle, and Laurie and my siblings. The day arrived when the little yellow slip in our box indicated we had packages to pick up. My husband was waiting for me in the car when I came out with the post office's little dolly filled to the brim with love. I took one look at my husband and burst into tears. I can't be sure, but I think I saw him crying too.

While the postal routine of hoping the machines were working every day we arrived didn't stop for weeks; the feeling that we were having Christmas every day continued.

Our daughter, Michelle sent us fans and an inverter and more fans.

Laurie and Shawn Miller sent us fans and an assortment of other things and kept on sending them. It should also be noted that Laurie brought so much with her on one trip, I was able to take a great many items to the Women's shelter, who is always in need of help—hurricane or no.

Dodie Jacobi sent dog and cat food and canned chicken. You'll see a pattern.

Peggy Kroesch sent fans and healthy dog food.

My siblings, well, my siblings sent fans, and chicken and dog food and lights and new sheets and towels and just kept sending it. I'm lucky to have some of the best siblings on the planet and going through this, only reinforced it.

And if you think others didn't offer; you would be wrong. SO many people messaged me and really wanted to try and help. At times, it was, in fact, overwhelming. People who know me, know one of my favorite movies is "It's a Wonderful Life" and its sentiment about friendship. You see no man (or woman) is poor who has friends. I am RICH beyond measure in that department. My daily trips to the post office only reinforced how lucky I am whether their machines were working or not.

Me arriving home with care packages!

Am I Coming or Am I Going?

The first of my friends to leave had announced it almost immediately. She surprised me. A senior citizen with a perennially sunny disposition; she and her husband had endured—what I can only describe as a horrific experience (and that's saying something). They had had a run of bad luck with landlords but this recent one during a Cat 5 hurricane "did her in" in her own words. I knew there would be more to come. Every individual had to determine, based on their life's situation. I knew that, and yet it felt like someone tearing off a bandage.....slowly. She had me come and take some of her plants that she wasn't taking with her. We also negotiated prices on other items she was leaving behind. I wanted to take them, but I felt like a vulture; picking on someone's bones. I am amazed at the breathtaking speed with which she was moving. She had lined up housing; moving their automobiles (one of the few things they were taking); flights---all within a few weeks after Maria. When the lady decided it was time to go; it was time to go.

I got a Facebook message from a cousin of one of my KC friends who had moved to the island to help open a restaurant. Her place was demolished. Her employer was gone, and her money was running down. She asks me first if I know of any place, she could get employment and, of course, the answer is no. Then she asks if I've heard about the mercy ships and how that works.

This was an oddity, in all I knew about hurricanes, I'd never heard of this. The government contracted with a cruise line to come to St. Croix and transport as many people as they could, off the island, free of charge. You had to be in dire straits (wasn't that everyone?) and needed to be able to prove it—not exactly sure how that ever worked.

In any event, word spread like wildfire when the first one arrived. Again, because there was no real way to receive communications; most of the details were carried word of mouth. My husband and I knew we were not going to leave. We were trying to put our house and our lives back together and doing it from the mainland, just didn't make sense. That said, we understood the trauma and sense of loss so many people were feeling. I really do believe that it was that sense of being untethered, during that period, that still haunts me. Nothing that we knew before Maria, a scant two weeks later, was the same.

The mercy ships were docking in Frederiksted and were supposed to come multiple times. But no one trusted that. That first ship caused unintentional panic as people arrived in droves and some were turned away. There wasn't a great deal of rhyme or reason as to how some people were selected. It was also an issue if you wanted to travel with a pet. Like some many hurricanes before; people were made to choose between their lives and the lives of their pets. Most tried to find friends or family to keep them "until they came back"; but most would never return.

The mercy ships continued until limited flights could resume at the airport—which also was crippled by Maria.

We helped friends with animals and transportation. Each friend or family that told us they were leaving; we'd pause and look at them and wonder if they knew something we didn't. Making the choice to go or stay was complicated for everyone; but our entire lives and livelihood was tied up in our choice to live on St. Croix. We never questioned the wisdom of it when we first arrived; but with each passing day, when we had a moment to reflect, I know we both did.

I was often asked why we didn't just pack up and leave and come back later. There is no real easy answer to that. If you think about people staying in the face of wildfires or mudslides or the flooding that can happen in so many parts of the continental US; I think you can find your answer. St. Croix was our home and whatever was going to happen; we knew we wanted to be a part of its rebuilding. It is also true that once everything started happening and we were working on the day to day; we really didn't have time to think about much beyond what was right in front of us. I also considered us extraordinarily lucky. If we had needed to get off island; we could have done so, and we had multiple offers of places to stay.

I had someone refer to us one time as brave. I don't think we were brave anymore than anyone else is that survives a natural disaster. Stamina, maybe. Brave, not so much.

While I was writing this, I had time to reflect on the friends I lost over Maria. Not their friendship but their physical presence. I treasure every memory I have of them. Maria took many things from me; but not my friends.

Beast of Burden

One of the saddest victims of hurricanes, to me, are the gentle souls—children, animals, the elderly. Left to fend for themselves; the hurricanes can reek incalculable horror.

Our animal shelter was an older campus, situated mid-island. It was made up of a series of small buildings, in a campus-like setting. It must be said that the employees there do God's work. They are overwhelmed, underpaid and, some days, under-appreciated. I have had friends who have volunteered there and heard the terrible stories of people who truly have no souls. How anyone could ever intentionally hurt a defenseless animal is so foreign to me. I don't now, nor will I ever get it.

Maria did some damage to the shelter, but not as much damage as the looters, who felt like they had to go back and loot the place more than once. Again, no idea why. The equipment was pretty old. The drugs were limited. In the end, it was just assholes who had nothing else better to do. Sorry, but that's just what it was.

After the final looting, the shelter was closed indefinitely. They needed to regroup, like everyone else and because the buildings were so badly damaged; they needed to find a place to relocate.

I need to back up here and tell you that before Maria, we had problems with stray animals. I'm told it's not as bad as other Caribbean islands (I've not been to them all) but a problem, nonetheless.

Prior to the arrival of both Irma and Maria, all the groups involved in animal welfare had pleaded with residents to bring their animals inside, even if they weren't inside animals; or, at a minimum, unleash them so they could find a place to shelter. Some did and some didn't.

What many people in the states have begun to realize is that lots of people think of their pets as family members and they don't want to be separated from them. I know people that pooled resources and chartered planes to get them and their animals off island. When the flights returned, some airlines were allowing people to bring their pets with them in the main cabin. So, people had some options.

As I mentioned in another chapter, some people left their pets with friends or other family members on island. Some people boarded them at the veterinary centers that had re-opened. To be sure, the options were limited and some, just cost prohibitive.

But then there were people who just did the worse thing. They left and left their animals to fend for themselves. A tenuous situation with our homeless animals became worse. You'd be driving down the road and see two or three dogs running together—scared and looking for food and some with collars, indicating that at one point, they were someone's pet.

I have tried very hard not to judge what drives people to abandon animals. If you've ever had a pet, you know the depth of their loyalty. Some of these poor creatures were scared and confused and trying desperately to find their families. If you've ever rescued an animal, it is simply heartbreaking to look into their eyes and see the sadness and fear because they don't understand what's going on.

I confess, I'm a bigger animal lover than most; but this dumping of innocent animals was a side of humanity I didn't want to see. So, where I could I started rescuing.

Let me say here that there are many and I do mean MANY more volunteers who behave selflessly every day on behalf of homeless animals. I was, what you would call, a newbie. But let me share one story with you.

I, like many others, started carrying dog food around in my car. Many animals, either abused or just too confused to understand were wary of anyone they didn't know—even if that stranger had food. So, most times, if they wouldn't come to me; I would simply throw out food and hope for the best.

One day, I was pulling into a store parking lot and I see a medium size chestnut colored female dog. It's getting near closing time and as the employees are streaming out; I begin to question each of them if they know the dog. Most shake their head at me but towards the last of the group, a man says that she'd been living there since the hurricane.

This was next to the main road that loops around the island and I knew there would come a point when she'd be hit by a car. Not if, but when.

So, I go into my car and pull out dog food and start tossing pieces to her. Like all the other dogs before her, she kept her distance although she did start looking at me as opposed to trying to run away. I couldn't catch her that day, but I felt (for reasons I didn't know) confident that I could catch her. Where I would take her after that; I hadn't a clue. But I'd worry about that later. I decided that day would be the next day.

So, armed with more dog food and a leash, I showed up the next day. I spent quite some time looking behind buildings and down alleyways until finally I spotted her under a car. She came out from under it when she saw me, but her guard was up. We spent some time like this—me throwing her dog food and her, inching closer to me. Finally, she was within my grasp and I quickly scooped her up. She was thinner than I realized and as I put her in the back of my car, she looked, momentarily, panicked.

Because the shelter wasn't open; my choices were limited. I couldn't take her home because my dog could be unpredictable around strange dogs. I drove straight to Sugar Mill Veterinary. When I walked in, the ever-amazing Liz, was behind the counter. I knew the policy was that the dog needed to be mine. So, I lied and said she was my dog. Liz was busy doing paper work and said, I'm sorry, we're completely full. I hadn't planned on that and I froze. Liz looked up and saw the expression on my face. Ok, I said she's not my dog, I just found her. But I'll pay to board her and pay for her treatment. I was having verbal diarrhea, but I was hoping if I just kept talking, she'd change her mind. While all this was going on and unbeknownst to me, the puppy was walking around behind the counter to Liz and went and placed her head on Liz's lap. Liz looked into her big brown eyes and said, "well she's as sweet as pumpkin pie". So began Pumpkin's odyssey.

It became evident, quickly, that she had been someone's pet. She walked well on a leash. She knew basic commands and she was house broken. But more than any other thing, she craved human touch. If you paused for five seconds walking her, she would stretch out her paws on your knee as if to say, please pet me.

Pumpkin stayed at Sugar Mill longer than I had hoped but because of the generosity of Molly and Ed Buckley, in opening their store to help find strays homes—Pumpkin found hers. It's not just anyone who will adopt an older dog. And while Pumpkin was cute as any puppy I'd seen; we just couldn't find her peeps. Until, one day, we did.

Kate and Eric saw in Pumpkin what I always saw—a loving, sweet dog, who wanted a family to call her own. I'm happy to report that Pumpkin is happy, healthy and continues to thrive. Her little family no longer calls St. Croix home (they moved to NY), but she is as lucky as any dog could be. And if you don't believe me; go check out her Instagram page—The adventures of Pumpkin butt.

Hurricane dogs and cats, as well call them, are still out there. All of us that live here, and love animals try not to focus on the losses and concentrate on the wins. If you get a chance to adopt one of these amazing creatures—run, do not walk to do so. I promise you'll never regret it.

Pumpkin, when I found her, eating the kibble I threw to her.

Pumpkin, on her way to meet prospective parents!

Pumpkin, just smiling and being her adorable self!

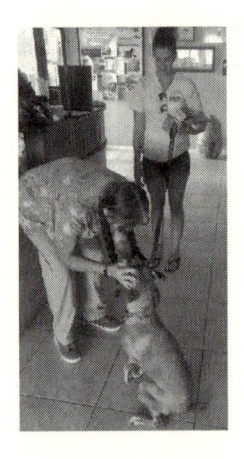

Pumpkin saying goodbye to Liz to leave with her new mama!

50 | Page

Relief Workers

After the linemen, the relief workers, were the ones that, for the most part, brought added value to the island. They did, of course, what you'd think they did—delivered water, aid, helped evacuate people that needed to be evacuated, etc. They came in all forms—government, private NGAs, religious organizations, the list goes on. I'm working on the assumption that most people understand the basic functions of these groups. If you've ever donated to the Red Cross; I don't have to explain it. So, I won't go into detail about that. What I'd like to share with you, is about some of the people.

There is a nice little bar/restaurant, at the end of our road called Castaways. Marne and Jesse are two of my favorite people on the planet (their daughter Lux is pretty high on the list too). What Castaways does is provide all ways to entertain yourself while you are eating and drinking. Bingo? Check. Open mic? Check. All types of local entertainment pass through their establishment.

A couple of things you need to know about Castaways. Maria took the beautiful Mahogany tree that graced the center of their establishment, sliced her up and then drove her through their roof for good measure. Marne and Jesse and their good friend (and bartender) Yeager were there the next day assessing damage. Frank and I happened to be in the area and helped them finish off various bottles of liquor as we helped them, literally, pick up pieces. They worked tirelessly to get their business back up and running and modified for the floor plan to accommodate the now, roofless bar.

Once they re-opened is when the relief workers really stepped up.

One of the casualties of vacation spots, following a natural disaster is the loss of tourism. While St. Croix has a bit more of a base of businesses then most islands; it is still a huge factor. When the restaurants started reopening, locals were certainly eating there, but it didn't fill the void entirely. (There's a reason a lot of them close during offseason.) The relief workers became substitute tourists. They ate dinners at local restaurants. They bought tickets for fundraisers. They bought gifts, clothing, etc. at local boutiques. If there was a place to support; they stepped. And here is my story of how I got to really appreciate the relief workers!

As mentioned, Castaways has an open mic night. It is always a busy night but while the relief workers were here and ESPECIALLY right after the storm, they were there in droves. They sang. They danced. They bought food and drink. Generally, they were the best 'tourists' ever. I remember one night; we were all feeling particularly blue. It was hot. Most of us had no power. We were just grumpy. There was a group of relief workers who didn't know each other but they bonded over music. They threw down riffs from the Allman Brothers to Bob Seger and everyone in between. There was so much dancing and laughing and drinking and laughing. We almost forgot for a moment the current state of our lives. We forgot the general misery and how far away normal would be. We just reveled in the happy state of being.

There are, at this writing, still a lot of relief workers on this island. Most of them are replacements for the others that had been here so long. But there are others who have been here since the beginning. Been here since we were all walking around, shell-shocked, at the current state of our lives. It's hard to describe what a few hours of escape can mean at this juncture; but I promise you, anyone who has gone through something like this, totally gets. So, to the relief workers—all of you, but especially the ones who played my favorite Eagles' song; you will always have a place on this island. And, even if you never come back here; we will always consider you one of us. Thank you, from the bottom of my heart.

The ABC's of Relief

If you have ever been in an area that is declared a national emergency, you will understand what I am about to say. It is convoluted. And that, is being kind. What is accessible, or should be, to you, right after these events, is FEMA. Remember, "you're doing a good job, Brownie"? Yea, that organization.

A couple of weeks into the hurricane follow up, we went to apply, like everyone for FEMA. We had long term issues we needed to address but we needed some short-term relief. We were denied the "initial" support of $500 that went to, I'm not kidding, everyone we knew. It was supposed to go to all residents (even though they say it doesn't) to help with initial expenses. Strike one against FEMA.

Then we decided we needed to apply with the SBA. The way the process worked was, if you qualified for FEMA but were turned down (for whatever reason) you should apply to SBA. Although their money wasn't free, it was at a significantly reduced interest rate. So, my husband and I packed up our documents and headed to the SBA center that was housed in one of the outbuildings associated with the fort in Christiansted. Un-air conditioned and small; it housed both SBA and FEMA. Each time you went in, no matter how many times you went and no matter if it was for the same thing, you had to register. This meant you had to provide your name and assigned number and why you were there. This was always the first line you encountered and there was no jumping it. Even if you were just dropping off a document, you had to register. It was the rule.

So, the first day that we were there, we had to sit in the line to register. That took about an hour. Once the registration was complete, we had to wait again, and that line was determined by whether you needed to see SBA or FEMA. One group went one way and the other group went the other. Once you were divided into your appropriate sides, you waited. Then you waited. And then you waited some more. After 3+ hours, we finally made it to the individual who was supposed to help us sort it out. At lease that's what he said he would do. It should be noted that we were hot, sweaty and still shell-shocked by the recent events. The SBA person was named, let's just call him, John.

John was a career employee of the SBA disaster team and he spent the first several minutes sharing with us his career with the organization. Then he spent the next 15 minutes complaining to us about the ship they were all living on.

Here, I need to explain. Because the entire island was without power and many of the hotels were damaged some or completely; there was no place to put all the workers that had arrived on the island. So, someone, I'm not sure who, had the brilliant idea to bring a cruise ship in and house them there. Everyone on the island, with, apparently the exception of John, thought it was a great idea. Remember that the cruise ship had power, air-conditioning, solid roofs, 3 meals a day and oh, did I mention power? You see John was upset, or so he told us, because every disaster he'd been sent to, he had been given a suite.

I would desperately like to tell you that I made this up. I did not. While an entire island just went through a Cat 5 hurricane and didn't have power (some didn't have homes); John was annoyed that he didn't have a suite.

My husband and I just looked at each other in disbelief. He reached over and patted my hand. I'm certain it was to keep me from saying something or leaping across the table and killing this imbecilic. But truthfully, at that point, I just didn't have the energy.

I ran into John multiple times after that and each time I went there, I studiously avoided him and went to whomever else was available. Surprisingly, I don't think he understood my avoidance. Maybe if he ever reads this book and puts two and two together—he'll figure it out.

And there's FEMA.

The Federal Emergency Management Association was created to help US citizens in times of disaster. I used to hear stories about how inept the organization was, and I thought it was exaggeration. I am here to tell you, it is not.

Let's first start with how it works. They have staff that sign you up in person, assign you a number and then, after that, they want you to do everything electronically. Think about that for a second. On an island, that has no power, they want you to find access to power (but not through them) and continue to monitor your case online. But what about if you don't have a laptop (not a rare thing). You can manage it through your smart phone (again assuming you have one). Piece of cake, right? Well that assumes that your phone provider is working. For several days, at one point, no one who had AT&T had service because some asshole stole the generator that ran the cell tower for the whole island. Yup, that is true.

But let's say the moon and stars align and you can access your account to try and file claims. Well then you must have copies of your receipts. You can take a picture of it with your phone but then it must upload to the system. Remember that no internet provider was working on the island. None. So, a simple one-page document to send could take 15-20 minutes. Easily. Then you had to assume that they got the document; it was filed and processed appropriately. Did. Not. Always. Happen.

I would not be lying if I said I could write a whole book on how badly this whole system was managed. But part of the reason I had high blood pressure during this time period was because of FEMA. At one point, we had given up hope of getting anything out of them and had just narrowed it down to reimbursement for a chain saw that we had to have shipped (you know to remove the trees so we could get out of the driveway), the generator we had to buy when our old one broke and fans. We had literally gone through many, MANY people to find out if this was allowable. I sent documents multiple times. I had even met a senior FEMA person who had family in Puerto Rico who had gone through Maria (sympathetic ear, right?) and he monitored our file. At one point, he told me to go into a FEMA center, ask for a certain document and fill it out. So, being the dutiful individual that I am, I did that. I ran into the buzz saw that is bureaucracy. I had the misfortune to meet (after I'd signed in again) a new FEMA supervisor who wanted to know why I wanted that document. Why was I getting help from someone not in St. Croix? Why did he tell me to fill out that particular document? I lost it. I just did. My level of anger and anxiety boiled over, and I lashed out. Before I was done, I was sobbing and everyone in the center was looking at me. I finally calmed down. She gave me the form and promised I would not have any more problems. She would personally see to it. She said to give it a few days to be processed but that this was the end of the road for my problems.

So, I waited 3 days (for good measure) and went on the FEMA webpage to check on our status. I punched in our number, which I now had memorized and it came back "no account existed". I stared at the blinking screen. I punched the number in again. The same error message. I was sitting in my car; at the only decent hotspot I could find; trying to understand how a government agency could cause this much grief and anxiety to people already suffering from grief and anxiety. I wanted to hurl the phone out the window, but I knew it was my only lifeline. So, I did the next best thing. I rolled down the window and screamed. It solved nothing but it made me feel better.

I went home and explained all of this to my husband and I said, "I will go through and do it all again, if you make me." The look on my face said I really didn't want to do it, but I would. He didn't make me and the circus that had become FEMA ended. Until it didn't. A few months after this, we get a phone call from FEMA asking if everything was going well and if we needed anything from them.

AND, I'm not making that up either.

Hurricane Drinking

Alcoholism runs in my family so the fact that I named this book Hurricane Drinking is not lost on me.

I have always been pretty conscious of my drinking habits (excluding college because, come on, it's college) but for the rest of my adult life, I have, shall we say, been aware. Drinking on island is always a challenge. I've seen many people move here and just lose their lives because, even though they are now living here, they think they are still on vacation and drink accordingly. That, my friends, is not sustainable. It happened to us initially. But like the island troopers that we became, we discovered the balance.

As you know, from other chapters, immediately following the hurricane, we were under a curfew. The non-curfew hours were from 12-4 every day. You had to do all your shopping, etc. during those four hours. You could (and they did) be arrested if you were on the streets during curfew hours. They were serious about it. So, left to our own devices, with limited power, no tv or internet, we fell back on the tried and true. We drank. We drank a lot.

One of the reasons that I've always been less excited about booze is the calories. But since we were off any semblance of a normal diet; I threw caution to the wind and started drinking.

On an island where two separate brand names of rum are produced –Cruzan Rum and Captain Morgan, it is an understatement to say that booze, specifically rum, is readily available. You can buy it in the hardware store for Pete's sake. It is plentiful and cheap. Rum here is cheaper than some bottles of soda. And that is not an exaggeration. So, accessibility was not an issue. We could get it.

When Jennie and Hop moved in with us, we raised our game and started drinking good, quality wine. They are both wine connoisseurs and it felt less like excessive drinking if it is a good bottle of wine. Since our evening always consisted of a good meal with the four of us; adding wine to the meal seemed a natural extension. And since we were just hanging out at the house before the meal, a before meal drink made sense. And, as you probably guessed, we couldn't go anywhere after the meal; a cocktail after the wine we had with the meal, followed. This didn't just become a routine. It became a habit.

The drinking also seemed to calm nerves and help, not just us, but everyone, who was in this, deal in a better way with the craziness that seemed to swallow us.

As I said in another chapter, we drank with our friends, Jesse and Marne, the day after the hurricane. We couldn't wrap our heads around the damage to their business, so we drank. It made, at least for a minute, things seem ok.

I don't want you to think that we only drank in bad times. We did some celebrating. Let's be honest here. We survived two Cat 5 hurricanes on an island 27 miles long and 6 miles wide. If that isn't something to celebrate, I don't know what is. We also celebrated the small things.

We celebrated birthdays. We celebrated Halloween. And, of course, every time someone's power came back on; it was a HUGE celebration.

One night, at Castaway's open mic, I decided to do something I hadn't done since high school. I decided I was going to sing in public, by myself. There is a reason they call booze liquid courage. It is just that. I had several cocktails and told the guy managing the program that I wanted to sing. Once I had committed, there was no backing out.

When I got to the stage; I said the one thing I had truly been thinking. After Maria, I wasn't going to let anything, including singing in public, scare me anymore. The crowd, survivors all, roared their approval. I also sang a song I knew my husband loved because I love him. I got through it and I think I did ok. The booze helped but candidly, that courage came from within.

As time passed and more and more of us got back online, it seemed that our drinking hadn't slowed down but more of our normal life was returning. My husband and I took a hard look at ourselves one day and said, we need to slow this train down. And so, we did.

Alcohol got us through so much. It got us through both hurricanes as they happened. It got us through the aftermath of Maria and the countless things, big and small, that made our lives miserable. It got us through problems we couldn't solve. It helped us laugh and it provided a salve for pain that couldn't be cured with an aspirin. In the end, it was what we needed at the time.

As I look back at those days, I see how much we drank. I wouldn't say we abused alcohol, but we certainly gave it a run for its money. I've no regrets. Everything happened in the way that it should for the times that we were in.

My step-daughter, Michelle and I have an expression that we use frequently. Everything happens for a reason. And I still believe that. I believe in my heart of hearts that even Maria happened for a reason. Not all those reasons are apparent to me yet; but I know they'll show up in time.

One thing I know for sure. Hurricanes will either break you or make you stronger. I'm happy to say I'm stronger. At least that's what I believe.

Epilogue

This book was something I felt I had to do. I had time to reflect and it helped that I had kept a journal during most of our ordeal. (It's why I had certain details so specific.) I'd like to tell you that everything is back to normal; but that wouldn't be true. Power has been restored to all the island, but it took several more months to get internet back to our house. We are now going on our third round of replacement electrical poles. Don't ask.

We have a new Governor who seems committed to help us move forward. He seems genuinely concerned about solving the problems of the past and finding a way to, if not protect us, then minimize potential impacts of weather events in the future.

My husband and I are getting our businesses back on track. When Irma hit St. Thomas and St. John, my business, Island Contessa, lost all my accounts on those islands, which was the bulk of my business. Some are coming back. Some will never return. I have good help and an amazing support system so it will be built back.

2018 was our 25th wedding anniversary and we decided to visit our friends from St. Croix, Kim Lucas and Chuck Ulrich, who have a place in Portugal. It was a beautifully relaxing trip with great friends, far, far away from the chaos that had consumed our lives for so many months.

We never did get any emergency government help although a local home repair program did resurface our roof. So, there's that.

Our insurance company, like many from Hugo, so many years ago, is on its way to bankruptcy—if, when this is published, it isn't already.

Life goes on, on my sleepy little island. Life goes on.

I have many people to thank.

First, my husband. My handsome, wonderful, patient husband. I would have never survived this, all of this without him. I love you, sweetheart. You make the world make sense.

Our family and friends. It was truly life affirming to get so much support from so many people. It would be impossible to list everyone because I would inevitably leave someone out; but you know who you.

And finally, to my island family. We got through this together. Stronger. More resilient. We really can take a beating and get up and go on. Let's just hope we don't have to test that theory for a while. I love you all.

Made in the USA
Columbia, SC
20 December 2024